W9-CHY-003

Sermon Outlines
From
Proverbs

by

Charles R. Wood

KREGEL PUBLICATIONS
Grand Rapids, Michigan 49501

Sermon Outlines From Proverbs by Charles R. Wood.
Copyright © 1984 by Kregel Publications, a division of
Kregel Inc. All rights reserved.

Library of Congress Cataloging in Publication Data

Wood, Charles R. (Charles Robert), 1933-
  Sermon Outlines From Proverbs

  1. Bible O.T. Proverbs — Sermons — Outlines, syllabi,
etc. I. Title
BS1465.4.W66   1984   251.'02   83-25569
ISBN 0-8254-4023-8

3 4 5 6 7 Printing/Year 91 90 89 88 87

Printed in the United States of America

Contents

Introduction

The book of Proverbs is a practical book within the confines of another practical Book. Its pages are filled with the lessons of life in the most understandable and applicable form. The book tells us how to live and enumerates the consequences of failing to do so.

The messages were prepared with living in mind, and each is designed to produce some tangible change in the living of the hearer. They have been carefully researched and prepared on the basis of the most likely interpretation of the individual passages. Each has been preached to the congregation of the Grace Baptist Church in South Bend, Indiana, and revised on the basis of the actual experience of preaching. They are the product of almost thirty years of preaching the Word.

These are expository messages in the main, designed to take the passage of Scripture and to draw out its message from the passage itself. In many instances the outline is based on the very words of the passage and the order in which they appear. Behind every message is the prayerful concern of a pastor's heart desiring the best for his people.

The messages appear in sufficient detail to be preached "as is", but they will be put to far better use if they are carefully studied with the text in hand and then adapted to the needs and personality of the specific congregation. The outlines are sufficiently detailed that, in some cases, portions of messages could be separated out and structured into complete sermons.

This task has been a labor of love on the part of one who loves the Word, loves preaching, loves preachers and loves the Church of Jesus Christ. They are sent forth with the earnest prayer that they may be used of the Lord to assist some of His servants in communicating the Word more effectively to the hearts of His people and thus building His church wherever it may be.

Weeping Wisdom

PROVERBS 1:20-33

Introduction:

We talk so much about obeying the Bible, but we do not always do much about it. We really ought to do more in actual practice because the Bible itself calls upon us to do so.

I. **Wisdom Weeping (vv. 20, 21)**
   A. Wisdom identified
      1. Personified — viewed as if human
      2. Actually found fully in the person of Christ
      3. Comes through prophets and teachers
      4. True wisdom is recorded for us in the Word — the Bible
   B. Wisdom located
      1. Out in the open: nothing necessary in divine wisdom is ever hidden
      2. Wisdom is where people are
         a. The message is clearer than we like to admit
         b. Most people know more than they like to admit

II. **Wisdom Warning (vv. 22-31)**
   A. Warning sounded (vv. 22, 23)
      1. How long?
         a. Will the simple (those ignorant through carelessness or indifference) love simplicity
         b. Will the scoffers (those who hold things in derision) delight in scoffing
         c. Will fools (those who hate knowledge because of its restraints) hate knowledge
      2. Call to repentance — "Turn and be helped"
         a. Turn when reproved (put self under my reproof)
         b. Be helped — if you will repent
            1) I will pour out My spirit upon you
            2) I will make known My words unto you (If we turn to God He will give us what we need to know and do. The usual reason for our confusion is failure to do right.)

7

B. Warning strengthened (vv. 24-31)
  1. Refusal (vv. 24, 25)
     a. I have called and reached out
        1) By preachers, etc.
        2) God has tried to get His message across
     b. I have been refused and disregarded (general tendency, especially among young, to disregard wisdom and instruction)
  2. Reaction (vv. 26-28)
     a. I will hold you in derision in time of need. (This is not as crass as it seems. He traces the reaction of wisdom as the results of rejection begin to work themselves out. Notice the strong words.)
     b. When they call in time of deep need, there is no answer because judgment is already falling
  3. Ruin (vv. 29-31)
     a. Fools have made their own choices (calamity is the result of their own ways). We often blame God for what we have done
     b. Fools have rejected attempts to help them
     c. Fools will get back the results of their own foolish choices and perverse ways
        1) Both in this life and the life to come
        2) Sowing and reaping prominent here

III. **Wisdom Weighing (vv. 32, 33)**
  A. Fools
     1. Destruction and ruin
        a. Their own choices destroy them (destroy themselves)
        b. Their own prosperity becomes their downfall (carelessness, unconcern, carnal security produced by worldly success)
        c. Rebellion against God chief cause
     2. They end up where they were heading
  B. Wise men
     1. Security and spiritual peace
        a. Listeners shall dwell safely (confidently)
        b. Listeners shall have quiet from fear of evil (note stress on freedom from fear)
     2. They end up where God has been leading them

8

Conclusion:

Wisdom continues to cry out — only in stronger and fuller form — the Word of God. Men, including Christian men, continue to ignore the cries and appeals of wisdom. Men especially turn away from the teaching of the Word.

There is always a balance beam. Every individual can climb on one side or the other. Will you hear, heed and follow, or will you close your eyes and ears and go your own way? The ultimate outcome is up to you. Throughout time and eternity you will reap the fruit of the decision you make now regarding wisdom.

The Godly Life

PROVERBS 2

Introduction:
The Bible is a practical book that really relates to life. Proverbs, many feel, is the most practical book within that practical Book. Proverbs 2 is especially practical. Here are six practical pointers:

I. **How to Find the Will of God for Your Life** (vv. 1-5)
   A. "Receive My words" (have a heart open to them)
   B. Keep them in your heart
   C. Listen for the teaching
   D. Determine to do what you learn and God shows you
   E. Diligently seek to know the wisdom of God. Then shalt thou know

II. **How to Recognize the Things the Lord Does for Us** (vv. 6-8)
   A. He gives wisdom
   B. He is the source of knowledge and understanding
   C. He rewards the righteous with wisdom
   D. He is a defense to those who walk uprightly
   E. He keeps the paths for those who want to do right
   F. He preserves (protects) the way of His people

III. **How to Identify the Benefits of Knowing the Lord** (vv. 9-12)
   A. An understanding of right things
   B. "Discretion (ability to distinguish) shall preserve thee"
   C. "Understanding will keep thee"
   D. "He will deliver from the way of the evil man"

IV. **How to Know What the Wicked are Really Like** (vv. 12-16)
   A. They speak froward things
   B. They leave the path of uprightness to walk in the way of darkness
   C. They delight to do evil
   D. They delight in the wickedness of others
   E. Their ways are crooked and perverse
   F. The evil woman is a "stranger"

V. **How to Identify an Immoral Woman** (vv. 16-19)
   A. A "strange woman"
   B. One who flatters with her words
   C. A forsaker of God
   D. One who leads to death

VI. **How to Experience the Blessing of Doing Right** (vv. 20-22)
   A. The upright
      1. Walk in the way of good men
      2. Keep to the path of the righteous
      3. Dwell (in safety) in the land
      4. The perfect (mature) shall have long life
   B. The wicked
      1. Shall be cut off from the earth
      2. The wicked shall be rooted out of it.

Conclusion:

The Christian has so many temptations. Here is a clear picture of right and wrong that will help us make our decisions, if we will only listen and heed through obedience.

How to Know God's Will for Your Life

PROVERBS 2:1-6

Introduction:

It has been said, "God loves you and has a wonderful plan for your life." In watching average Christians, one sometimes wonders if most have any idea about the truth of a wonderful plan for their lives. How about the will of God for your life? Have you found that wonderful plan, and are you living according to it?

I. **The Need to Know God's Will**
   A. Human experience shows us:
      1. Messed up lives
      2. Mixed up marriages
      3. Unhappy personalities
   B. The Bible shows us:
      1. That which is "perfect, good, acceptable"
      2. That which can be known
      3. Two specific areas
         a. God's directive will
         b. God's permissive will

II. **The Finding of God's Will** (vv. 1-6)
   A. The steps to knowing:
      1. Put a priority on God's Word (v. 1)
         a. Hide it in safe custody
         b. The Word of God is the only source of revelation
      2. Be sincerely open to what God has for you (v. 2)
         a. "Sharpen your ear"
         b. "Turn your heart" covers the internal, intellectual, emotional aspects
      3. Earnestly pray for God to reveal it to you (v. 3)
         a. Earnestness goes beyond sincerity
         b. The passage speaks of "Cry" and "Lift your voice"
      4. Sincerely seek it through every possible means (v. 4)

a. Persevering, unrelaxing — seek — dig for truth
b. The Word is superior, but it also can show in conviction, circumstance, etc.
B. Promises of provision
1. Discernment and discovery promised (v. 5)
2. Promises come from the One who gives

III. Hindrances to Knowing God's Will
A. Self-will — do not really want to know His will as it might conflict with my own
B. Indifference — do not really care
C. Elevation of feeling above fact
1. Desire for some "special feeling" — this obscures the will of God
2. Stress on having to follow feeling rather than fact
3. Allowing feeling impressions to dominate
D. Failure to do what we already know of God's will
1. Many common examples
a. Children obey parents
b. Parents discipline children
c. Do not marry the unsaved
d. Immorality is wrong
e. Be a witness — seek to win people to Christ
f. Tithe
g. Walk with the Lord
2. Your failure to know God's will may really be a refusal to do it!

Conclusion:

It is so crucial that you find the will of the Lord!

His will involves your salvation. "He is not willing that any should perish..." (1 Peter 3:10).

You must start at the beginning by being sure you know His salvation.

How to Be Afraid

PROVERBS 2:1-9

Introduction:

The writer of Proverbs speaks of "the fear of the Lord." That basically means to know the Holy One. It involves knowing Him personally. It brings a sense of reverential awe. It results in a proper ordering of our lives.

But how can we get to know Him in this way? We know the first step is saving faith. This passage, among other things, talks of getting to know Him better.

I. **The Quest (vv. 1-4)**
   A. The conditions
      1. "If thou wilt receive:" to receive graciously and openly
      2. "If thou wilt lay up:" to file something in a safe place such as the memory, the conscience, the heart
      3. "Incline thine ear:" sharpen your ear — so that it hears better
      4. "Apply thine heart:" to turn the heart in a direction (tip it over)
      5. "Cry" — "lift up the voice:" words which indicate intensity of approach
   B. The summary — (verse 4 caps it)
      1. "Seek as silver" — refers to mining operations Persevering, unrelaxing and diligent
      2. "Searchest . . . as for hidden treasure"
      3. There is a quest involved in coming to know the fear of the Lord

II. **The Reward (vv. 5, 9)**
   A. Promise at end of quest — know the fear of the Lord
   B. Other good things go along with this
      1. Certain characteristics
         a. "Righteousness:" that which is right or straight (esp. morally)
         b. "Judgment:" delivery of a correct judgment on human activities

14

           c. "Equity:" demeanor or honorable action on our part (has meaning of equal — balanced scale)
      2. A course of life — "every good path"

III. The Results (vv. 6-8)
    A. Wisdom, knowledge and understanding are assured
       1. These are results of the fear of the Lord
       2. These are the gift of God
    B. Certain other benefits are assured
       1. "Sound wisdom" — wisdom which always has soundness
       2. He provides a protection for His people
       3. He keeps men walking the right path
       4. He guards, protects, etc., the way of His saints

Conclusion:

How does one come to know the Lord? It is a divine gift in response to human effort, but we can be more specific. The knowledge of God is a divine response to human effort invested in the Word of God (cf. vv. 1-3, 6). The more we know the Word, the more we know the Lord; but it must be a matter of heart and head (cf. v. 2). Knowledge of the Lord brings wisdom with all its benefits — (cf. vv. 7-9), especially a well-ordered life and walk.

Understanding Life

PROVERBS 3

Introduction:
Proverbs 3 contains ten practical lessons that Christians need to know to help them understand life and to avoid the pitfalls along the way of life.

I.   **How to Live a Long Life (vv. 1-4)**
   A. The key
      1. "Forget not My law"
      2. "Let thy heart keep My commandments"
      3. "Let not mercy and truth forsake thee"
      4. In other words: internalize your beliefs
   B. The benefit
      1. Quantity of life — length of days and long life
      2. Quality of life
         a. Peace
         b. Favor with God and man
         c. Good understanding with God and man

II. **How to Know the Guidance of God (vv. 5, 6)**
   A. "Trust in the Lord with all thine heart"
   B. "Lean not to own understanding"
   C. "In all thy ways acknowledge Him"
   D. "He shall direct thy paths"

III. **How to Avoid Spiritual Sickness (vv. 7, 8)**
   A. "Be not wise in thine own eyes"
   B. "Fear the Lord"
   C. "Depart from evil"

IV. **How to Get What You Need (vv. 9, 10)**
   A. The command
      1. "Honor the Lord with thy substance"
      2. "With the firstfruits" (stress promissory nature)
   B. The reward
      1. "Barns filled with plenty"
      2. "Presses bursting with new wine"

V. **How to Handle Troubles** (vv. 11, 12)
    A. Commands
        1. "Despise not the chastening of the Lord"
        2. "Do not be weary of His correction"
    B. Reasons
        1. "The Lord correcteth whom He loveth"
        2. He treats us in father/son relationship

VI. **How to Understand the Importance of Wisdom and Knowledge** (vv. 13-24)
    A. Their effect — happiness (blessed)
    B. Their value
        1. Their worth — above riches
        2. Their benefit — long life
        3. They bring pleasantness and peace
    C. Their possession — don't let them get away
    D. Their benefits
        1. Help the walk
        2. Give safety

VII. **How to Be Not Afraid** (vv. 25, 26)
    A. Things not to fear
        1. Unexpected calamity
        2. The desolation brought on by onslaughts of the wicked
    B. Reasons not to be fearful
        1. The Lord Himself is your confidence
        2. He will keep your foot from being taken

VIII. **How to Deal With a Bountiful Hand** (vv. 27, 28)
    A. Command
        1. "Withhold not good from those to whom it is due"
        2. When you have the power to do it
    B. Illustration
        1. Don't make your neighbor come back again
        2. If you can deal with the matter today

IX. **How to Get Along With Others** (vv. 29, 30)
    A. "Devise not evil against a neighbor"
    B. "Strive not without a cause"

X. **How to View the Wicked** (vv. 31-35)
  - A. "Envy not"
  - B. "Choose not His ways"
  - C. Agree with God's analysis of him and his ways

Conclusion:

A practical book has practical truth for our daily lives. These ten steps will lead to success, especially to spiritual success. It is not enough to write them down or even to memorize them. We must put them into practice in our daily lives.

What to Do When You Do Not Know What to Do

PROVERBS 3:5, 6

Introduction:

We are so often faced with things for which we are not really equipped. Many problems leave us fractured. The pressures of life mount up, and we lose our orientation. We so often hear, "I do not know what to do."

What should you do when you do not know what to do? Here are ten suggestions —

I.   **Walk Closely With the Lord**
     A. Maintaining daily fellowshp with Him will help in time of need
     B. Make a regular practice of turning everthing over to Him

II. **Take the Matter to Him in Prayer**
     A. Do not ever do anything without His guidance
     B. Do not fail to do anything He shows you to do

III. **Don't Try to Figure Things Out on Your Own — "Lean Not on Your Own Understanding"**
     A. Unaided reason will always lead to more problems
     B. It is not wrong to use your reason
        1. So long as it is not your reason *alone*
        2. Reason must be submitted to the will of God

IV. **Submit Yourself and the Situation to His Will**
     A. Be willing no matter what His will may be. "If any man will do His will, he shall know of the doctrine" (John 7:17)
     B. Do not try to predetermine or "rubber-stamp" His will

V.   **Clearly Express Your Problem**
     A. Put it in writing
        1. Helps to clarify it

      2. We sometimes find answers while stating the problem

   B. Be sure you really have a problem
      1. Sometimes our only problem is worry
      2. Some problems are not worth having

VI. Search for Bible Principles
   A. If there is no direct teaching available
   B. Try to find principles that apply
      1. Why it is important to express the problem clearly
      2. There are principles for every situation

VII. Be Sure There Is No Sin or Disobedience Involved
   A. "If I regard iniquity in my heart..." (Psalm 66:18)
   B. Sin blocks
      1. Not doing what we know we should while seeking to know more
      2. Broken fellowship prevents answers
   C. Sometimes our problem is that we know the answer, but we just will not act on it

VIII. Seek Godly Counsel
   A. Cautions
      1. Do not go to those you know will agree with you
      2. Do not seek too many
   B. Why it helps
      1. Others may have been through the same thing
      2. The uninvolved see more clearly

IX. Do Not Act Until You Have to or Until You Know What to Do
   A. Often we do not have answers because we do not need them yet
   B. Many situations care for themselves or provide their own answers

X. Expect God to Give You Direction
   A. Move on — do not let it stop you
   B. This verse is a promise

Conclusion:

Here's what to do when you do not know what to do.

These steps can help you do something about the tough situations and keep you going until you find the solutions God has for you.

Avoiding Spiritual Sickness

PROVERBS 3:7, 8

Introduction:

There is more than one way to get sick. You can get physically sick, but you can also get spiritually sick. Spiritual sickness is often far worse as it affects that part of us that will live forever. Here are some tips on how to avoid spiritual sickness.

I. **"Be Not Wise in Thine Own Eyes" (v. 7)**
   A. Do not be impressed with yourself
      1. Nothing uglier than the pretty girl who knows it
      2. Nothing dumber than the intelligent one who knows it
   B. Do not be closed to instruction
      1. Learn from your critics
      2. Listen to your teachers
      3. Find some models on which to pattern your life

II. **"Fear the Lord" (v. 7)**
   A. Basic meaning
      1. Hold God in awe
      2. Old Testament term for salvation
   B. Further implications
      1. Need some fear of the Lord in the sense of being afraid of what He can do
      2. Remember
         a. God sees everything you do
         b. God knows everything you think
         c. God knows everywhere you go
      3. You will answer for all the above, in the judgment

III. **"Depart From Evil" (v. 7)**
   A. Turn away from doing evil
      1. Other side of doing right
      2. Avoid every potentially evil situation
   B. Stay away from the evil man (vv. 31-35)
      1. Envy him not
      2. Choose not his ways
      3. Agree with God's analysis of him — he is wicked and a fool

Conclusion:

A good spirit in any group depends on the members of that group. The success of any enterprise also depends on every person in the group. Spiritual sickness will "take you out of the play." Resolve to stay healthy by avoiding spiritual sickness.

Attending God's School

PROVERBS 3:11, 12

Introduction:
These verses are an expanded quote of Job 5:17, and they summarize and explain the whole book of Job. Verse 11 traces Job's problem, and verse 12 has his answer to it. These verses, however, explain far more than Job. They explain the whole realm of problems, afflictions, etc., and show us how God wants us to handle them.

I. **Attitude**
   A. The proper understanding of chastening
      1. Its nature is schooling
      2. This involves chastening and all problems, etc., that come our way
   B. The proper response to chastening
      1. Despise not the chastening of the Lord
         a. Do not view it resentfully
         b. Do not fail to pay it heed
         c. Do not fail to learn from it
         d. Do not dread God and His dealings
      2. Be not weary of His correction (Hebrews 12:5, 6) ("faint")
         a. Do not judge amiss the Father's dealings
         b. Do not neglect present duty
         c. Do not cherish morbid brooding over sorrows
         d. Do not refuse to be comforted
      Summary: No matter what comes in God's school, we are not to despise it nor faint under it.

II. **Assurance**
   A. Chastening is correction
      1. God is not necessarily punishing us; He is trying to correct us
      2. It is the correction of the family, not the school or prison
   B. Chastening (correction) is a sign of God's love
      1. It is a sign of sonship
         a. There can be no closer relationship — correction is an integral part

          b. He that escapes affliction may well question his adoption

      2. He only corrects those whom He loves

  C. Chastening (correction) is for our good

      1. It is designed to "straighten us out"

          a. To make us like what He wants us to be

          b. To keep us from the harm of evil

      2. It has specific purposes

          a. It is individual — to show us our corruption

          b. It is educational

          c. It is tailored to our needs — Adam's self-will, pride, independence, waywardness — and designed to break our negative traits

      3. It is handled perfectly by God

          a. The fittest time

          b. The surest, gentlest means

          c. The most considerate measure

          d. The most effective instruments

Summary: We can bear up properly under chastening because we have these three great assurances: it is correction; it is a sign of God's love; it is for our good

III. **Applications**

  A. Honor God with everything

      1. Honor prosperity by giving of your substance (vv. 9, 10)

      2. Honor chastening and affliction by giving your submission

  B. Seek to avoid the necessity of chastening

      1. Watch for first whispers of His will

      2. Look for intimations of His providence

      3. Seek the guidance of His eye

  C. When it comes, accept it as part of the relationship

      1. Reverence it as a sign you are under His hand

      2. Expect a rich experience of His sustaining grace

      3. Do not look at the rod; look at the hand that wields it

  D. Examine every trial to see if there is correction in it

      1. Not all His classes are corrective

      2. Each should be examined

      3. Seek to determine what is being corrected

      4. Act upon it immediately so it can stop the pressure

E. Keep faith in time of affliction
   1. Understand why He chastens — to correct
   2. Acknowledge it as part of His gracious dealings with you

Conclusion:

The pain of suffering sometimes keeps us from seeing what God is doing in our lives. Sometimes He melts us in the furnace so He can stamp us with His own image. He wants us to partake of His holiness so we can partake of His happiness. If we compare our chastening with our sin, is it not a marvel that it is not heavier?

Withhold Not/Want Not

PROVERBS 3:27-30

Introduction:
Our mothers used to say, "Waste not, want not." It was a good saying, but the Bible goes far beyond that. The Bible takes us into realms where we do not want to go. It gets to meddling around with money, possessions, etc. Much Christianity stops short of that area. Let's let the Bible speak for itself.

I.   **A Principle Stated (v. 27)**
    A. The command — "Withhold not"
       1. Do not fail to do
       2. Do not hold back from
    B. The identification — "Good"
       1. That which helps, assists, builds up, contributes to
       2. Goes far beyond money
         a. Actual physical assistance
         b. Encouragement
         c. "Know how"
         d. Your presence and participation
    C. The limitations — up to this point very general
       1. "Them to whom it is due"
         a. Someone who has earned it
         b. Someone who has a desperate need for it
         c. Someone who is worthy of it
         d. Rules out some
            1) The Bible sets up principles on this — rules out the lazy, loafer, freeloader, etc.
            2) Means we should not help in some situations
            3) Some basic rules
               a) The person who works or seeks to work steadily
               b) The person who practices biblical principles
               c) The person who uses what he has wisely
               d) The person who assists others — the obligation of the poor to give to the poor
       2. "When it is in the power of thine hand to do it"

        a. When you have it to do with (we are never expected to give what we do not have — so long as God agrees that we do not have it)
        b. When your own obligations are current
           1) Not necessarily "paid up"
           2) Unless God clearly shows otherwise

II. The Principle Illustrated (v. 28) (just one application)

A. Do not turn your neighbor aside
    1. Do not send him away to return another day
    2. Your reasons are crucial
        a. If you hope matter will be forgotten or dropped
        b. If you hope it will be covered by another
B. If you can help him now, do so
    1. A little given in time of need is worth more than the same amount given later
    2. Reasons
        a. The person may be beyond your reach tomorrow
        b. Tomorrow is the province of God
        c. The need may be increased by delay
        d. God always says "now"

Conclusion:

We should be looking for opportunities to do good. Sowing and reaping keep us from running out.

Are you doing good to all around you who are deserving? Are you withholding? (Proverbs 11:24, 25)

Keep Thy Heart

PROVERBS 4:23

Introduction:
Did you ever wonder why a person dies? It is always because his heart stopped beating (although there will be something that caused it to do so). How significant that heart truly is! The Bible recognized that significance a long time ago.

I. **The Command — "Keep Thy Heart"**
    A. In Hebrew the heart is the "kernel of the nut;" the internal citadel of the soul
    B. The command means it *can* be done
        1. All excuses are removed
        2. If God says "Keep it," then it can be kept
    C. The command means it *must* be done
        1. This is not presented as an option if you would like to work on it
        2. We are responsible to do it
        3. We must determine how to do it

II. **The Cause — "For Out of It Are the Issues of Life"**
    A. The heart controls all of life
        1. The vital spring of the soul
        2. The fountain of all actions
        3. The center and seat of all principle
        4. The heart controls actions; actions determine habits; habits are the structure of character
    B. The heart is so easily taken
        1. Satan sets a constant watch on it — if he can get "a piece of the action," he can regain some lost ground
        2. It is so easily deceived (Illustration: Ananias & Sapphira, Acts 5:3)
        3. It is hard to position
            a. A heart not settled
            b. A heart not "in it"
            c. A heart not right
    C. The heart is so easily covered. There is the danger of conformity when the heart is not in it — sooner or later it comes out

D. When the heart goes down, the total man goes down

III. **The Challenge — "With All Diligence"**
   A. Essential meaning — with all keeping. "Before all else that you have to guard"
      1. Our greatest attention should be given to the heart
      2. "Closely garrisoned" (as you would protect the source of your drinking water)
   B. Every inlet of sin must be strongly guarded
      1. Note following verses (vv. 24-27)
      2. "Make no provision for evil"
   C. The heart must be kept in specific ways
      1. First, it must be surrendered to God
         a. That is the problem of many hearts
         b. Rebellion makes the heart impossible to keep
      2. Then diligence in what is put in it
      3. Then saturation with the Word
      4. Then a will to pray

Conclusion:
   Keep your heart, because it is the starting point for just about everything in life. Sinful actions almost always begin in the heart. Every man, even every godly man, has some tendency to moral weakness, some weak point, a sin-opening in his moral armor. Keep your heart!

The Cure for Heart Trouble

PROVERBS 4:23-27

Introduction:

Heart disease is a great killer taking hundreds of thousands of lives annually. Heart disease is an enormous problem among Christians because it takes its toll of spiritual lives and vitality. Proverbs speaks of heart trouble, but it is better than medical science, for it proposes a cure.

I. **Commandment**
   A. The object — "thy heart" — used 90 times in Proverbs
      1. Defined: the whole inner nature: the life of thought, feeling and will
      2. Illustrated: Arabic cognate word is "lubb" — the kernel of the nut
   B. Action — "keep" (v. 23)
      1. Definition: guard, preserve — keep out rather than in
      2. Implication: positive steps are to be taken in regard to the heart; take great care what you allow into it
   C. Intensity — "with all diligence"
      1. Translation: "Guard thy heart above all other things to be guarded"
      2. Priority
         a. There are many things we watch carefully
         b. Above all these, set yourself to watch your heart

II. **Reason**
   A. The inner self (heart)
      1. Likened to a fountain
      2. Out of it, all of life issues — the stream which comes out of the fountain of the heart determines the course of life
   B. It has a flow
      1. Likened to heart pumping blood to the body
      2. Currents of moral life flow out of heart

C. It makes determinations
   1. The condition of the heart determines the outflow of the fountain
   2. The actual course of life is determined by the state of the heart

III. **Method**
   A. How does one keep the heart?
      1. Heart determines conduct; conduct determines heart
      2. Heart determines what you will be (especially involuntary and unpremeditated spontaneous acts); but you must determine what your heart will be
   B. Steps to a guarded heart
      1. Controlled speech (v. 24)
         a. Meaning
            1) A twisted mouth — that which twists or misrepresents
            2) Perverse lips — that which bends aside — falsehood
         b. Implications
            1) Don't engage in this or have anything to do with it. Stay away from these kinds of people
            2) Speech is the index of the mind
      2. Controlled motive (v. 25)
         a. Meaning
            1) Not likely referring to physical eyes
            2) Has reference to moral goals
         b. Applications
            1) Fix your moral gaze straight ahead — deals with motives, purposes, aims, desires
            2) Become goal-oriented morally
            3) Keep motivations straight
      3. Controlled conduct (vv. 26, 27)
         a. Meaning
            1) "Ponder" — means to remove impediments to the level and smooth
            2) "Established" — fixed, set, stable
            3) "Turn not" — keep on course
            4) "Remove" — keep away from

b. Applications
1) Pay attention to moral conduct
2) Keep your life lined up with the above principles

Conclusion:

It is so important to safeguard your heart properly as all of life — actions, words, etc. — issues out of it.

Cautions Against Sin

PROVERBS 5

Introduction:

This chapter speaks against adultery, but it has far broader applications. The area of morals is one on which today's Christian needs much help. There are, however, some general principles here which refer to sin in general rather than just the specific sin of adultery.

I.   **Sin Is Always Bitter/Sweet (vv. 3, 4)**
  A. Sin always appears good and fun when first introduced
   1. There must be some appeal to it
   2. Sometimes its forbidden nature is its greatest appeal
  B. Sin always has a hidden bitter side
   1. Sin in the collective always appears worse than in the specific
   2. Careful observation shows its real nature

II. **Sin Is Best Handled by Avoiding It (vv. 8, 9)**
  A. It is easier to avoid it than to extricate yourself from it
   1. This is obvious on the surface
   2. Experience proves it
  B. Many cautions involved
   1. Beware of where you walk, look, etc.
   2. Beware of the people you let get close to you
   3. Beware of where you turn in joy, sorrow or trouble

III. **Sin Always Exacts Its Price (vv. 11-14)**
  A. Element of certainty
   1. Very often long delayed (to give us an opportunity to get turned around)
   2. The penalty often comes in gradual degrees (unrest, depression, etc.)
  B. The penalty may come in various forms or combinations
   1. Physical price (v. 11)

      2. Gnawing remorse (v. 12)
      3. Realization (v. 14)
      4. Mental anguish

IV. **Sin Draws Us From the Things Already Ours** (vv. 15-17)
   A. Sin involves rejection of what we have
      1. Sin says that what God has given us is not enough
      2. Sin often results from failure to realize what we have
   B. Sin always involves loss of what we have
      1. Based on last principle
      2. Many of today's youth are losing more than they realize

V. **There Is No Place Secret Enough to Commit Secret Sin** (v. 21)
   A. God's omnipresence and omniscience makes this sure
      1. Why do before God what you would not do before men?
      2. What is done before God is done before the One who can punish
   B. Interesting comparison here
      1. God sees men's ways and judges them
      2. If our eyes are closed, God's will not be; if we open our eyes, God will close His

VI. **The Price of Sin Is Being Released to Sin** (vv. 22, 23)
   A. God sometimes delivers men to sin
      1. Clearly seen in drug addiction
      2. This is worse than being exposed or overtaken by the law (The worst thing that can happen is to be allowed to sin without correction)
   B. Man sometimes deceives himself
      1. Always sure he can extract himself
      2. Few ever make it

Conclusion:
The double life is a dangerous and risky one to live. May we develop such an understanding of and aversion to sin that we are never guilty of living in such a way.

Not Slothful in Business

PROVERBS 6:1-19

Introduction:
In order to honor the Lord in our business lives and dealings, there are four ingredients which must be present:

I. **Independence (vv. 1-5)**
   A. Situation (v. 1)
      1. Never become surety for someone
      2. The modern counterpart — co-signing, etc.
   B. Sentence (v. 2)
      1. You are caught in a trap
      2. Your own words and commitments have snared you
   C. Solution (vv. 3-5)
      1. Get yourself out of the relationship
      2. Use any and every legal means to do so

II. **Involvement (vv. 6-11)**
   A. Consideration (vv. 6-8)
      1. Go to the ant and observe her ways
      2. Take careful note of her industry
   B. Challenge (v. 9)
      1. How long will you lie sleeping?
      2. When will you get up and get moving?
   C. Condition (vv. 10, 11)
      1. Continued sloth and unconcern will lead to sure failure
      2. Poverty and want will surely come to the lazy

III. **Integrity (vv. 12-15)**
   A. Description (vv. 12-14)
      1. Wicked man speaks lies
      2. Wicked man acts out lies
      3. Wicked man thinks lies
   B. Destination (v. 15)
      1. He will come to calamity
      2. He will ultimately end up broken

C. Determination
   1. Set yourself to avoid his ways
   2. Determine to escape his end

IV. **Innocence (vv. 16-19)**
   A. Condemnation
      1. Things God hates
      2. Form of poetic repetition — does not make the seventh one worse
   B. Clarification
      1. "A proud look" — high, haughty arrogance
      2. "A lying tongue" — one habituated to untruth
      3. "Hands that shed innocent blood" — lack of concern for the welfare of others when on a quest for self
      4. "A heart that deviseth wicked imaginations" — one whose heart and mind are given over to sin and filth
      5. "Feet that are swift in running to mischief" — one who has a tendency to find evil and get involved!
      6. "A false witness that speaketh lies" — one who lies concerning another person and thus bears false witness
      7. "He that soweth discord among brethren" — one who goes about setting people at odds with each other

Conclusion:
Inclusion of concern for these four areas in our business dealings will go a long way toward producing success in God's sight!

Your Father and Mother's Bible

Introduction:

The passage speaks of the father's commandment and the mother's law. These two things refer to the instruction, based upon the Word of God, given by parents. They actually can be taken to refer to your parent's Bible (the place where the commandment and the law are found).

I. **The Command (vv. 20, 21)**
   A. The object in view
      1. "Thy father's commandment — Thy mother's law"
      2. This means the commandments and law that are held precious by your parents
   B. The steps to be taken
      1. "Keep" — adhere to earnestly
      2. "Forsake not" — do not turn aside from
      3. "Bind them upon thine heart" — come to know them so well that they become part of your life
      4. "Tie them about thy neck" — let your knowledge of and adherence to God's Word be your chief ornament

II. **The Reasons (vv. 22, 23)**
   A. The threefold benefit of the Word
      1. Guidance — "When thou goest, *it* shall lead thee"
      2. Protection — "When thou sleepest, *it* shall keep thee" (If you have built the Word into your life, it will have created the lifestyle and responses necessary to cause safety when you are not in control of the processes of life)
      3. Provision — "When thou wakest, *it* shall talk with thee" (The Word hidden in the heart will communicate and bring thoughts to mind of a beneficial nature).
   B. The three-fold description of the Word
      1. "A lamp" — that which provides clarity and illumination

2. "A light" — that which clarifies and brightens the path
3. "Way of life" — reproofs of wrong conduct and positive instruction keep one in the pathway leading to life

III. The Result (v. 24)

A. It will keep from evil
 1. Evil in general and as a principle
 2. No better way to avoid evil than through the Word
B. It will keep from a specific evil
 1. It deals with an immoral person
 2. No better protection in moral realm than the Word!

Conclusion:

The Word of God is the key to successful living. Make sure that its commandments and precepts are the daily guide for your life. Study them, know them, and live them.

The Good Life

PROVERBS 7:1-4

Introduction:

We often say, "This is the life." Life has many meanings, but we all know what is meant by "the good life." Most of us really want to live it, but how many of us are really doing so?

I. **An Appeal**
   A. Commercials present us with the "goods" necessary to the good life as the world sees it
   B. This essentially involves an appeal to the physical, tangible, sensuous
   C. Hedonism (love of pleasure) is the order of the day

II. **An Alternative**
   A. Deals with Hedonism (love of pleasure and self) beginning at 6:20
      1. Certainly speaking specifically of immoral woman here
      2. Surely speaking of much more — represents all sensual appeals
   B. Shows foolishness of this evil
      1. Adultery
      2. Immorality in general
      3. Writer clearly rejects Hedonism as pathway to real living

III. **The Answer (7:1-4)**
   A. Principle: Keep My commandments and live
   B. Method: Keep the commandments of the Word as
      1. A man keeps his money — "lay up"
      2. A man protects his eye — "apple of the eye"
         a. "Little man in the eye"
         b. Lamentations 2:18; Deuteronomy 32:10; Psalm 17:8; Zechariah 2:8
      3. A priest keeps the law — "Bind them" Deuteronomy 6:8
      4. A man loves his family

C. Rationale
   1. Society says let go — the Bible says hang on — how can it be
   2. Answer lies in these ramifications
      a. The world was created perfect and would have led to the good life
      b. Sin's intrusion brought suffering, sorrow, death
      c. The commandments of the Word are designed to break sin's power
      d. The less we live under sin's hold, the more likely we are to have the good life

Conclusion:

We want the good life, and we miss it. Usually it is not because of major sin, but an accumulation of a myriad of small matters. We need to major on the Word of God to keep us from sin so we can live the good life.

Isn't It Great to Be a Christian?

PROVERBS 10

Introduction:

We often hear the above question. Sometimes we may wonder — what is really so great about that? This chapter lists scores of reasons. Let us look at just a few.

I. **The Christian's Soul Will Always Have Sufficiency (v. 3)**
   A. Can always be sure of a "fed soul"
      1. So much soul emptiness
      2. Accounts for enormous suicide rates
   B. Actually refers to other needs as well (Psalm 34:9, 10; 37:25)

II. **The Christian's Head Is Covered With Blessings (v. 6)**
   A. The "just" is the one who knows the Lord
   B. Blessings are too many to count
   C. Sometimes we may need help in recognizing blessings, because we tend to miss them.

III. **The Christian's Mouth Becomes a Source of Life (v. 11)**
   A. "Well" — source of something
   B. Emphasizes witnessing

IV. **The Christian's Desire Shall Be Granted (v. 24)**
   A. Speaks of things his heart really wants
   B. Touches the realm of prayer
   C. This is an area completely unknown to the world

V. **The Christian's Days Are Lengthened (v. 27)**
   A. His knowledge of God extends his days
      1. This is generally speaking
      2. Statistics bear this out
   B. This is a result of biblical principles
      1. The things we sometimes resent become our blessings
      2. Obedience bears its own reward

VI. **The Christian Is Able to Make Proper Use of His Mouth**
   A. The mouth is a problem to so many people (v. 6)

B. The Christian has wisdom to speak (vv. 13, 31)
C. The Christian also can keep quiet (v. 19)
D. The Christian utters precious things (v. 20)
E. The Christian's words provide food for others (v. 21)
F. The Christian's words are well-ordered and planned (v. 32)

Conclusion:

The next time someone says, "Isn't it great to be a Christian?", you should be able to say a strong, "Yes!"

Weights and Measures

PROVERBS 11:1

Introduction:
The Bible is such a practical book and has so much to say about the ordering of our daily lives and affairs. This verse is one of the most practical in the Bible as it deals with the details of daily living.

I.   **Its Meaning**
   A. Understand the Hebrew system of weights and measures
      1. Balance beam
      2. Use of stones of various sizes
      3. It was convenient and accurate
   B. The false balance
      1. There was a standard weight deposited in the sanctuary (2 Samuel 14:26)
      2. "Balances of deceit"
         a. An altered balance beam
         b. Shaved or tampered weights
      3. An abomination to the Lord — God has His reasons
         a. It violates His commandments (Deuteronomy 25:13-16; Leviticus 19:35, 36)
         b. It debases the orderly operation of society
         c. It degrades the man himself -- no man can rob another without injuring his own soul
   C. The just weight
      1. "A stone of completeness" — "A full stone"
      2. Includes both balance beam and stone
      3. Is a delight to the Lord

II. **Its Spheres**
   A. Initially commercial
      1. Israel very commercial at this point in history
         a. Note other commercial references (6:1; 16:11; 20:10; 20:23)
         b. With commerce always go dangers of dishonesty

      2. Later abuses showed how much this material was needed
  B. Essential part of society's structure
      1. Proverbs was for the instruction of the young
      2. It is useless to raise the structure of national religious life without first laying the foundation of common honesty
  C. Operated in a broader area
      1. Commerce among Israel was all among brothers
      2. This teaching would really apply to all relationships among brothers (or between man and man)

III. Its Implications
  A. Our relationship to God is such that it is all encompassing
      1. Commerce is included in the rightful place of Christianity
      2. There is nothing in the life of a Christian outside the sphere of God's control
  B. Honesty and integrity are at the very foundation of life
      1. "Honesty is the best policy," should be "honesty is the biblical policy"
      2. That which is hurtful to others is hateful to God
  C. God wants us to give full measure in all we do
      1. Note that the balance and weights were not missing — just short
      2. We tend to give short measure in many relationships
         a. Marriage partners
         b. Children — parents
         c. Workman — employer
         d. Christian to Christian
      3. Our worst area is in our relationship to Christ
         a. We give short measure most of the time
         b. Anything less than our best is a "balance of deceit"

Conclusion:
God extends His controls to every area of our lives. Honesty and integrity must be at the foundation of those lives. We must give full measure in all our dealings.

Hanging By an Exception

PROVERBS 12:15; 26:12

Introduction:

Have you ever wondered how people can do some of the incredible things they do? Some are incredibly bad (by people who are good). Some are incredibly stupid (by those smarter). Some are incredibly out of character. I think I have found the answer. It isn't because people are deliberately bad or just want to see how much they can mess up. There is another reason behind it.

I.   **We All Believe There Are Rules in Life**
   - A. We know that life works that way
     1. Certain things should always be done
     2. Things should be done in certain ways
   - B. We all know and operate by many rules
     1. They have been presented since childhood
     2. They become part of the fabric of life
   - C. We are in basic agreement with rules
     1. Believe we must have them
     2. Basically accept the bulk of them
   - D. We all hold some of the rules very firmly
     1. Everyone has his own set of dearly held rules
        a. Something where we have no problem
        b. Something where we have won a great victory
        c. Something where we expect trouble
     2. Somehow these rules are held above all others

II.   **We All Know There Are Exceptions to the Rules**
   - A. Almost every rule has its exception
     1. Many times they just appear to be exceptions
     2. Many surely are commonly held as exceptions
   - B. Abuses of authority become exceptions
   - C. "Exceptions prove the rule"
     1. Not a correct statement
     2. Exceptions prove the humanity of those involved
     3. Exceptions prove the sinfulness of the world in which we live where nothing is fixed

III.   **We All Make Too Much of the Exceptions**

A. We seize upon them
   1. When something comes right home to us (We believe in the rule until we violate it and then claim that we are the exceptions)
   2. When it touches someone near us (Proverbs 26:17)
   3. When we do not understand what is going on
   4. When we do not know all the facts in a situation (We somehow have the idea that ignorance or confusion is a great excuse for not doing what we should do)
B. The harm this does to us
   1. The exceptions are very few
   2. The exceptions seldom really pertain to us — we think they do without really knowing what is involved
   3. The exceptions become a form of excusing and of blame-shifting
   4. The exceptions simply tend to confuse the issue
C. The price we pay for the exceptions
   1. They keep us from facing issues we should face (Why face the wrong if you are an exception?)
   2. They divert our attention from our real problems (They become like a most unfortunate shield held in front of us)
   3. They prevent God from working in our lives (He can not get through the exceptions to show us what He wants us to know)
   4. They result in protracted immaturity (We never come to the maturity God has for us, because we never really deal with the issues of life)
D. The cure for the exceptions
   1. Face the issue first
   2. Search your heart for wrong
   3. Deal with your own problems instead of always trying to get everyone but yourself straightened out
   4. Let God handle the rest — He can take care of it far better than you

Conclusion:

We — or what we have done — always turn up as the exception. Even the rules we most believe in do not apply when the "chips are down" and the pointer is on us. We need to change our approach.

Have a Good Day!

PROVERBS 12:25

Introduction:
We all have responsibilities to others. Everyone says, "Have a good day!" Are they wasting their breath? There is a sense in which Christians ought to be saying this every day to each other.

I.   **The Bane of a Heavy Heart**
    A. Practical experience
        1. Can make us feel awful
        2. Can reduce our effectiveness to nothing
    B. Biblical expression
        1. Heaviness weighs down (Proverbs 12:25)
        2 Can result in broken spirit (Proverbs 15:13b)
        3. Can affect physical health (Proverbs 17:22)
    C. Evident causes
        1. Melancholy temperament
        2. Specific problems
        3. General circumstances
Whatever the causes, etc., the heavy heart is an enormous burden

II. **The Cure for the Heavy Heart**
    A. Essential cure lies within
        1. Sometimes circumstances cleaning up can lift the load
        2. Usually some internal problem involved
    B. Many times an external force may begin the cure
        1. May take professional help in some cases
        2. Sometimes something much simpler involved
    C. Bible illustrates
        1. Proverbs 12:25 — A good word makes heavy heart glad
        2. Proverbs 17:22
          a. Not just for the individual
          b. Can be a medicine for others

III. **Our Obligation to the Heavy Hearted**
    A. We are commanded to bear one another's burdens, and this includes the emotional as well as the physical

B. Method
 1. Try to give others the benefit of doubt
 2. Try to maintain a cheerful approach
 3. Seek from the Lord the gift of the proper word (Isaiah 50:4). Translate: "That I may know how to sustain, with words, him that is weary"
C. It becomes a spiritual obligation
 1. James 2:14-16 — refers to the physical realm
 2. Should it any less refer to the spiritual and emotional realms?

Conclusion:

Have a good day! A snappy cliche or a sincere, earnest wish for someone? An empty statement or a real heart's desire?

The Anatomy of Riches

PROVERBS 13:17

Introduction:

There are so many confusing things being said about riches. There are those who teach that riches are a sign of spirituality, and there are those who teach that the two are totally unrelated. It is well to see what the Bible says.

I. **Interpreting the Verse**
    A. Initial meaning is to make one's self rich
    B. Secondary meaning
        1. The idea of feigning or masquerading
        2. It gives an idea of making one's self appear to be rich
    C. Both meanings can properly be used on the basis of other Scripture
        1. There is difficulty in determining which is correct
        2. Nothing definitive in the text

II. **Applying the Verse**
    A. The meaninglessness of outward appearance
        1. This is the secondary meaning
        2. It states an obvious truism
        3. There is a great spiritual truth involved (1 Samuel 16:17)
        4. It is an area in which we are often very guilty
    B. The relativity of standards of wealth
        1. Men's needs vary greatly
        2. The relative value of wealth varies greatly between God and men
        3. The result is that prayers, etc., are affected
        4. We need to tune our value systems to that of God
    C. The crucial importance of what is done with wealth
        1. Note that a man "maketh himself" something
        2. This is the whole thrust of Matthew 6:19-24
        3. This determines whether or not riches are right. "Riches are more justly determined by their use than by their possession."

      4. This may somewhat determine whether or not we have riches

D. The rewards of a proper attitude toward riches
    1. God promises future rewards for proper use of riches
    2. There are rewards at present (Philippians 4:11; 2 Corinthians 6:10; 1 Timothy 6:6)
    3. A man can truly "make himself rich" by "making himself poor"

E. The emptiness of man-made riches
    1. A man can make himself rich but have nothing
    2. This involves failure to understand the nature of true riches
    3. Some of the world's richest men are its poorest

F. The unimportance of wealth in relationship to riches
    1. Poverty and wealth are unrelated terms
    2. The poorest man in this world may be the richest one

Conclusion:

When you study the anatomy of riches through a verse such as Proverbs 13:7, you really begin to realize that things are not as they seem.

The Way It Seems

PROVERBS 14

Introduction:
  We say "Things are not always what they seem," and "Appearances are deceiving." If you watch today's world, you surely form some strange impressions. A lot of what is going on is not what it seems to be. Let us look at some of the impressions and the realities behind them.

I.   **"It Does Not Matter How You Live" (v. 2)**
  A. Current philosophy
    1. Division between life and belief
    2. Life-style and belief tend to be unrelated even for a Christian
  B. Biblical teaching
    1. There is a specific connection between life and belief (outward conduct shows inward feeling)
    2. Conduct shows the way in which we regard God
    3. A man is evil because he has cast off fear of the Lord
    4. If your belief does not change your life, there is something wrong with your belief

II. **"Sin Is Funny" (v. 9)**
  A. Current philosophy
    1. Commit sin lightly
    2. Give light names to serious transgressions (alcoholism = sickness)
    3. Pass over rebuke with a joke
    4. Much humor based on sin
  B. Biblical teaching
    1. Sin is funny — only a fool laughs at it
    2. There is a reversal here — sin mocks fools
    3. Sinner making a sin offering is a fool
    4. God is pleased with the righteous, not with sin!

III. **"Happiness Is Found in Doing Your Own Thing" (v. 14)**
  A. Current philosophy
    1. Restraint is the cause of unhappiness
    2. Complete freedom leads to happiness

B. Biblical teaching
  1. The determination to do one's own thing demonstrates backslidden condition
  2. We reap the fruit of what we sow
  3. The good man is filled with the fruits of his own life

IV. "Hard Work Is Not Worth It" (v. 23)
  A. Current philosophy
    1. "Don't sweat it"
    2. If it is too hard, do not bother with it
  B. Bibical teaching
    1. All honest industry has a reward
    2. Work was present even before the fall
    3. Language of action more eloquent than language of words
    4. Contrast with those who talk much and do nothing

V. "Say What You Think" (v. 33)
  A. Current philosophy
    1. Outspokenness is a virtue
    2. Best to say all that we think
  B. Biblical teaching
    1. "Anger withdraws the light of understanding"
    2. "He who is short in temper is a mighty fool"
    3. Proverb says — person telling all his mind is revealing his total folly
    4. A wise man does not blurt out all he knows

VI. "There Are Many Ways to Please God" (v. 12)
  A. Current philosophy
    1. There are many ways to get to God and heaven
    2. Postpone serious consideration of eternity
    3. Do not worry about it — we're all going the same way anyhow
    4. Tendency to judge end of road by its beginning
  B. Biblical teaching
    1. This is a warning against following an uninstructed conscience; must be informed by God's Word

2. Following a false light will lead astray
3. It "seemeth right" — men go along assuming they are right, when in reality they are not
4. Man makes the judgment, and he is not the final judge
5. We do it God's way or we die!

Conclusion:

Our society is so messed-up that we can almost teach, that if society teaches it or supports it, it is wrong. Most of modern philosophy in the world is dead wrong. The Bible counteracts all this and gives you something to go by.

There Is No Other Way

PROVERBS 14:12-16

Introduction:
The Bible often uses contrasts to make things stand out more clearly. The Book of Proverbs is dominated by the contrast between the wise man and the fool. Look, with me now at one place of contrast (verse 15).

I.   **The Simple Believeth Everything**
    A. Definition
        1. He is gullible, undiscerning
        2. "The fool goes running after everything that comes along"
    B. Grave danger in this
        1. Because there is a way that seems right but ends in death (v. 12)
            a. It looks right as well as good
            b. Its travellers often have arguments for going in that way
            c. Others point the way to it
        2. Because there is a laughter that ends in sorrow (v. 13)
            a. Fun on surface — misery underneath
            b. "Mirth that ends in heaviness"
        3. Because the backslider shall be filled with his own ways (v. 14)
            a. Backslider: fool who is gullible
            b. He ends up getting what he wants
        4. Because the fool rageth and is confident (v. 16)
            a. The more a man goes on in a wrong way, the more sure of himself he becomes
            b. The fools runs after whatever goes by and gets in big trouble because of the dangers that lurk for him

II.   **But the Prudent Man Looketh Well to His Going**
    A. Definition: the wise man weighs with care the way he is going
        1. He studies before following

      2. He tries to see the end before beginning
      3. He looks at those already on the way
      4. He compares the way to the Word
   B. Results
      1. He is satisfied from within himself (v. 14b)
         a. He has inner satisfaction
         b. He does not depend on externals
      2. He fears and departs from evil (v. 16b)
         a. He knows what evil will do
         b. He keeps away from it

Conclusion:

There are two kinds of people: the foolish and the wise. They do two kinds of things: run after whatever goes by and weigh carefully where they go. There are two ways to go: the way that seems right and the way that is right. If you go any way other than God's, the end is death; the mirth is sorrow; the reward is unrestraint; the attitude is arrogance. There is no other way than God's.

Evil Plowing: Evil Praying

PROVERBS 15:8, 9, 26; 21:4, 27; 28:9

Introduction:
When I was a boy, I tried to avoid unpleasant jobs by pleading problems. Dad would say, "You're really in bad shape." I really was not, but there are many who are. These may be people you would not suspect.

I. **In What Condition Are They?**
   A. They are unable to please God
      1. They do not satisfy Him
      2. They actually are an abomination to Him: "hateful" — a strong word
   B. Areas involved
      1. Commercial life (21:4) — has to do with earning a living
      2. Life in general (15:9) — refers to the whole course of life
      3. Thought life (15:26) — all thinking included
      4. Religious life (15:8) — all religious observances
      5. Personal devotional life (28:9) — all prayer is wrong
   C. This person is in tough shape: everything he says, does or thinks is deeply unsatisfactory to the Lord

II. **Those Who Are in That Condition**
   A. The wicked (15:8, 9, 26; 21:4, 27)
   B. The contrasts
      1. Wicked/upright (15:8)
      2. Wicked/follower after righteousness (15:9)
      3. Wicked/pure (15:26)
   C. The identification
      1. Anyone who is not righteous
      2. Righteousness comes from God
      3. God gives righteousness in Christ
      4. Anyone who has not accepted Christ as Savior
   D. Defined
      1. Not just "evil, wicked, vile people"

2. Anyone who has not accepted God's righteousness as provided in Christ is among the wicked in this section. The unsaved are the wicked

III. Why They Are in This Condition
A. Not because of
   1. Wrong opinions
   2. Serious mistakes
   3. Occasional or frequent transgressions
B. But because they have refused to do things God's way
   1. They have determined to withhold themselves from His service
   2. They hold they have the right to determine their own lives in their own way
   3. They thus deliberately ignore His will
C. Thus they live in
   1. Fixed rebellion against God (if God says you must do it a certain way, and you do not, that is rebellion)
   2. Settled disavowal of His claims
   3. Neglect of His holy law (you can not keep His law without accepting His righteousness. Sounds harsh and strong, but it is biblically true, and just a bit of logical thinking will confirm it)

IV. How to Escape This Bad Condition
A. Recognize the facts
   1. There is only one way to do things — God's way
   2. If you have not done it God's way, you are a rebel and therefore wicked
   3. Nothing you are doing is pleasing to God
B. Do things God's way
   1. Confess your sinfulness
   2. Recognize the righteousness God has promised
   3. Accept that righteousness by trusting Christ
C. See your responsibility to others
   1. We have been lulled to sleep
   2. Others are in wickedness
   3. We must reach out to them

Conclusion:

No one is in as rough a shape as the person outside of Christ. The worst tragedy is that it is so easy to escape, and so few actually do. Will you now turn from wickedness to Christ?

The Christian Virtue of Friendship

PROVERBS 17:17

Introduction:

In our stress on great theological themes and timeless moral principles, we sometimes neglect the simpler, more practical, things so essential to spiritual life. One of the Christian virtues which the Bible stresses is that of friendship. God uses this to illustrate the relationship between Christ and the believer, so it is very important. Someone has said, "A friend is one who comes in when the whole world has gone out." Aristotle said, "What is a friend? A single soul dwelling in two bodies."

I.   **True Friendship Is Independent of Temporal Factors**
    A. It is not limited by space
    B. It is not limited by time

II.   **True Friendship Is Independent of Circumstances**
    A. "A friend loveth at all times"
       1. Does not mean continual effusion (effusiveness is no proof of sincerity)
       2. Does mean — no matter what the circumstances
    B. Loveth — shows his love or makes it manifest
       1. Real friend shows that he loves
       2. This demonstration is for all times and seasons

III. **True Friendship Is Not Shaken by Slander**
    A. A true friend does not react to what he hears, etc.
    B. Explains teaching of verse 9

IV.   **True Friendship Is Made Stronger by Adversity**
    A. Clarified meaning
       1. Friendship moves into brotherhood at time of trouble
       2. Or friendship becomes brotherhood as a result of adversity
    B. First preferred but both true
       1. Friends can become closer than brothers
       2. Adversity becomes the measure of friendship

V. **True Friendship Seeks Its Object's Best Interests**
   A. Real friendship is not always agreeable and positive
   B. Thoroughly biblical (Proverbs 27:6)

VI. **True Friendship Is Not Broken By Self-Revelation**
   A. Definition — allowing one's self to be known
   B. True friendship not altered by seeing one at his worst

VII. **True Friendship Comes to Those Who Can Show It**
   A. People worry and fret about not having friends
   B. Bible says that friendship begets friendship (Proverbs 18:24)

VIII. **Christ Is the Perfect Example of True Friendship**
   A. Views us as friends
   B. He related to people as friends

Conclusion:
How do you do on friendship? Let us follow Christ's examples.

That Old Tongue

PROVERBS 18

Introduction:
Proverbs is a practical book which deals with the realities of every day life. Because of this, we can expect it to deal in "problem areas." One of the most frequent subjects in the book is the tongue. This is because it is such a frequent area of problem. This chapter points out three crucial factors about the tongue.

I. **The Tongue of the Wise Man (v. 4)**
    A. Obviously speaking of a good man
    B. Words are like deep waters (Idea: strong man has deep waters running in him. The lips express the heart and thus become springs)
        1. Proverbs 20:5
        2. Proverbs 16:22
        3. Proverbs 10:11
    C. Second phrase
        1. Proper translation: the well-spring of wisdom as a gushing brook
        2. Meaning
            a. The tongue of a good man pours forth as a fountain the words which express the deep waters within the man
            b. The mouth of the good man is a blessing to all around as is the gushing mountain stream

II. **The Tongue of the Foolish Man (vv. 6, 7, 8, 13)**
    A. Gets him into trouble (vv. 6, 7)
        1. He enters into contention
        2. His words call for stripes — not that he calls for them to be delivered, but that he ends up with them coming (19:29; 10:13; 26:3)
        3. His mouth brings him to destruction
            a. He is constantly in trouble because of his words
            b. He is gradually led down a perverse path
            c. This sometimes results in immediate destruction

4. His talk can hurt his soul
   a. Soul has reference to his spiritual life
   b. Sometimes people hurt their own spiritual lives with their loose talk (criticism, bitterness, sinful conversation)

B. Deals in poison (v. 8) (See 26:22)
  1. Translation: words of a whisperer are a dainty morsel
  2. Meaning
   a. "Whisperer" — one who tells things that can not be told out loud
   b. "Dainty morsels" — idea of easily swallowed
  3. Tragedy
   a. These things are easily accepted
   b. They become almost impossible to get rid of (correction does not always work)

C. Shows its folly (13)
  1. Answering before hearing
   a. This refers to cutting in before speaker finishes
   b. This involves answering before hearing the whole or both sides of a story
  2. It has its consequences
   a. Makes a man a fool
   b. Is a *shame* (disgrace) to him
  3. It is most common and most serious

III. The Important Issue of the Tongue (v. 21)

A. The tongue has death and life in its power
  1. The wise man uses his tongue to bring life and point men to it
  2. The foolish man's tongue obscures life and keeps men from it, thus inclining them toward death

B. They that use it much must live with its consequences
  1. We need to face this before using it (meaning of James 3:1)
  2. Illumines a passage such as Galatians 6:7

Conclusion:

"Watch your tongue." It is good advice.

Watch Your Mouth

Introduction:

We often use the phrase "Watch your mouth." To do it literally, you need either a mirror or to be crosseyed. But there is an important spiritual truth in that statement. Your mouth can do so much harm that you need a constant watch on it.

I. **Your Mouth Tells What You Are (v. 2)**
   - A. Rephrase: a fool does not want to learn anything; he just wants to express his opinions
   - B. Teaching (cf. 12:23; 13:16; 15:2)
     1. Listen to speech and learn what a person is
     2. A person always expressing his opinions may well be a fool (especially when his opinions are baseless or contradictory)

II. **Your Mouth Gets You Into Trouble (vv. 6, 7)**
   - A. Gets you into troubles which are not yours
     1. "Taking up another's offense" (26:17)
     2. Makes problems worse
   - B. Makes you "overspeak" — ask for punishment
   - C. Creates destroying strife — hurts you as much as the other
   - D. Hinders spiritual growth

III. **Your Mouth Makes You Enemies (v. 8)**
   - A. Rephrased: "The words of a gossip are like choice morsels; they go down into a man's inmost parts."
   - B. Teaching
     1. Gossip appears good and is avidly eaten
     2. It goes down to deepest levels and lodges
     3. It becomes more than it was intended to be
     4. Its effects can never be completely removed, and it will come back to haunt you

IV. **Your Mouth Tends to Move Too Quickly (v. 13)**
   - A. Don't speak until you have heard the whole story

      1. Giving advice

      2. Taking sides

  B. Give others the same benefit you want them to give you (the verdict should never go beyond the evidence)

V. Your Mouth Has Mighty Power (v. 21)

  A. Your speech can do great good or great harm

      1. More people have been killed by the tongue than by the sword

      2. Enormous responsibility rests in our tongues

  B. Use it and eat its benefits and curses

      1. Sowing and reaping comes in

      2. Use it wrongly — get it back wrongly

Conclusion:

Watch your mouth by resolving:

1. Not to talk so much
2. Not to take up the offenses of others
3. Not to gossip
4. Not to speak until you are sure you know the whole story
5. Not to use your mouth wrongly lest it bite you

The Importance of Obedience

PROVERBS 19:3, 16, 21, 23

Introduction:
There is great rationality in obeying the Word of God. This passage gives several very good reasons for doing so.

I.   **Keeping Commandments Keeps One's Own Soul (v. 16a)**
  A. "Commandments" has reference to the Word of God
    1. Specific things
    2. General principles and precepts
  B. "Keeping the soul"
    1. Preserving one's own spiritual welfare
    2. The ways involved
      a. Keeping the Word prevents sin's breach of fellowship
      b. Keeping the Word avoids stifling sense of guilt
      c. Keeping the Word prevents damage to conscience

II. **Keeping Commandments Is the Way to Real Life (v. 23a)**
  A. "Fear of the Lord"
    1. Awe, respect
    2. Used here in sense of obedience
  B. The tendency toward life
    1. Moves us away from things harmful to life
    2. The Commandments are designed to produce life
    3. In this direction lies satisfaction
      a. Explains why so many Christians are not satisfied
      b. A very practical matter that needs application

III. **Keeping Commandments Keeps Us Out of Way of Evil (v. 23b)**
  A. No visitation of evil
    1. Out of realm where the evil one works
    2. Saturated with that which arms against evil
  B. Explains some things
    1. This is a promise
    2. Things seemingly evil come into believer's life
    3. They are not really evil but intended for good

IV. **Failure to Keep Commandments Tends to Death (v. 16b)**
   A. This speaks of man "careless" about his ways
      1. The man who takes no heed to the course of his life
      2. The one who is careless about the commands of the Word
   B. This man tends toward death
      1. Spiritual death in the sense of damaged spiritual life
      2. Potential physical death from harmful practices, etc.
      3. Mental, moral and emotional death

V. **Failure to Keep Commandments Results in Dissatisfaction (v. 3)**
   A. Man's foolishness turns his way aside
      1. Most disobedience to the Word is man's folly
      2. This turns man away from what he should be and do
   B. His heart gets involved
      1. He loses peace in his heart
      2. He often turns on God
         a. Begins to blame God for his problems
         b. The person grounded in and obedient to the Word seldom turns against God as a result of adversity

VI. **Failure to Keep Commandments Is Folly for God Is Going to Have His Own Way Anyhow (v. 21)**
   A. Man has all kinds of ideas and plans
      1. Man tends to go his own way
      2. He tends to think he can run his own life
   B. The Lord's will is done anyway
      1. This is an ultimate, overall matter
      2. We just butt our heads against reality

Conclusion:
   Why should I order my life by the Word of God? Here are six excellent reasons.

Godly Counsel

PROVERBS 20:18

Introduction:
To say that we are human is to say that we have problems. They take so many forms. So often we need someone to talk with about them. We do not really want or need professional/pastoral counsel; none is available, or our problem is not that serious. We feel awkward about the whole thing. We need some kind of counsel!

I. **Why Should We Seek It? (Proverbs 20:18)**
   A. The biblical command
   B. Because others know more than we
      1. From experience
      2. From working with people
   C. Others are less involved and thus may see more clearly
   D. Others can help us work through our own confusion
   E. Others do not have the blind spots we develop (Proverbs 12:15)

II. **To Whom Should We Turn? (1 Thessalonians 5:12-14)**
   A. It depends on the nature and extent of the problem
   B. Available resources
      1. Professional — always begin with pastor
      2. Family — mate/parent
      3. Friends
      4. Other Christians
   C. Strong biblical case for counseling one another

III. **What Kind of Person Do We Want for Our Counselor? (Romans 15:14)**
   A. Is the person genuinely spiritual?
      1. Is he following biblical roles and patterns?
      2. Is he living according to the Bible?
   B. Is the person confidential? (You might as well put your problems on TV as to tell them to certain people)
   C. Has the person shown success in area where counsel is needed? (Do not ask someone who is bankrupt for financial advice)

D. What about the person's children? (A problem in one area is likely a symptom of or will affect other areas)
E. Does the other person have the same problem or perhaps a worse one? (Misery loves company nowhere more than in counseling)

IV. **Dangers In Seeking Counsel (2 Corinthians 10:12)**
A. Looking for a rubber stamp or approval
B. Not hearing what we are actually told
C. Turning to the wrong kind of counselor
D. Not identifying the real problem
E. Waiting too long to get help
F. Getting too much counsel (confusion)
G. Wanting answers, not solutions

V. **How to Become a Good Counselor (Colossians 3:12-16)**
A. Put on godly virtues (Christian living)
B. Put on love
C. Let the peace of God dwell in your heart
D. Be thankful
E. Let the Word of God dwell in you richly (The better you know the Word, the more effective you will be as a counselor)

Conclusion:
Many in the Bible sought good counsel (Moses/Jerusalem Council). Some did not (Rehoboam — 1 Kings 12:8). It is biblical to counsel and to seek it. Are you seeking in the right way in the right places? Are you able to counsel anyone else biblically?

An Old-Fashioned Christian

PROVERBS 22:28

Introduction:
This verse refers to stone pillars and other markers set up to denote land boundaries. Removal of them could have resulted in chaos for everyone. There are other landmarks, those which our fathers have set up, which are removed only at great jeopardy.

Our world has changed much and become very "modern." Some things are really out of style. Included is old-fashioned Christianity. How could you tell an old-fashioned Christian if you did find one?

I.   **He Believed the Bible**
    A. He knew it was God's Word
    B. He never dreamed anyone would say it had errors in it (He didn't know what inerrancy was, but he believed it)
    C. He took what it said as being so (regardless of opinions)
    D. He obeyed it completely
        1. What it forbade, he didn't do
        2. What it commanded, he did

II. **He Took His Christianity Seriously (2 Corinthians 5:17)**
    A. He realized there was something different about a Christian
        1. He was not afraid to be different
        2. He sometimes emphasized the outward rather than the inward, but he was more concerned with pleasing God than men
    B. He tried to live by the Bible all week long
        1. He was not a "Sunday only" Christian
        2. He did not have a compartmentalized or fragmented life
    C. He saw the importance of the church
        1. He attended no matter what adverse circumstances came up

2. He made it the center of his life (born, married, buried)
   D. He sought to tell others about Christ

III. **He Held to So-Called "Traditional Values"**
   A. It is more important to be right than popular
   B. He did not try to make two wrongs into a right
   C. He believed he should work for a living
   D. He did not need a contract: he bought what he could afford and paid his bills
   E. He stuck to one woman for one lifetime
   F. He loved his freedom enough to fight for it
   G. He kept his word
   H. He had a hatred for sin
   I. He had a love for things of the Lord

IV. **He Reared His Children Properly**
   A. He had not heard of a man named Spock
      1. He was not impressed by psychology
      2. He did not worry too much about phases
   B. He used the rod when necessary
      1. He helped his children
      2. He did not have to worry about a baby killer accusing him of child abuse
   C. He demanded that his children do right
      1. He made them do so
      2. He had not heard that he could not force them to do right
   D. He taught them to work and to respect authority

V. **He Believed Earnestly**
   A. All men are sinners by nature
   B. Sinners go to hell
   C. Christ died for us
   D. We must trust Him to go to heaven

Conclusion:
   Old-fashioned Christianity was not bad at all. In fact, we could use a good deal of it today. Are you an old-fashioned Christian?

Give Me Thine Heart

PROVERBS 23:26

Introduction:

There is nothing more important than the heart! The Bible makes much of it, and we would be wise to do so also.

I. **The Heart As the Core of the Person**
   A. It refers to innermost personality
   B. It also involves the emotions and affections

II. **Various Teachings on the Importance of the Heart**
   A. It can be "given" to someone or something such as:
      1. A person
      2. A place
      3. A career
      4. A thing
      5. A philosophy
      6. A job
      7. A desire
   B. Every heart is fixed somewhere
   C. It is so important where it is fixed
      1. The fix of the heart determines what he views as important
      2. The fix of the heart determines priorities
      3. The fix of the heart becomes basis for his actions

III. **God's Appeal**
   A. It is a command
   B. It is an invitation
   C. It is an appeal

IV. **The Problem of Giving the Heart**
   A. It is easy to assent to this
   B. It involves specific tangibles
      1. The problem of the spiritual versus the practical
      2. The passage deals with the inward and outward
      3. We somehow fail to bridge the gap
   C. God wants your heart and through it your conformity to His will

Conclusion:
Who has your heart? If God really has it, it will show itself in life.

The Peril of Neglect

PROVERBS 24:11, 12

Introduction:

About 90% of all the people won to Christ are won by 5% of professing Christians. If everyone sought to win souls the way you do, would you be saved today? Most Christians *never*, ever win a soul to Christ. Unless you have, don't argue with that statement.

I.   **The Crime of Negligence**
      A. A commandment is given
      B. It has a specific meaning
         1. Refers to those in jeopardy of any sort
         2. It has many potential meanings
      C. There is a pertinent application
         1. Who is closer to death and being slain than the unsaved?
         2. It would clearly command us to pay attention to the lost
      D. God commands deliverance attempts — failure is a moral crime

II.   **The Excuses for Negligence**
      A. We normally claim ignorance, but ignorance is no excuse
      B. Our real reasons lie in other areas:
         1. Sinful indolence
         2. Careless indifference
         3. Criminal callousness
         4. Selfish self-absorption
         5. Crass familiarity
         6. Vitiating procrastination

III. **The Condemnation of Negligence**
      A. God knows the weakness of our foolish excuses
      B. There is condemnation in the very descriptions used of God
         1. "He that weighs [sifts] the heart"

> a. He watches the heart carefully — we
>   superficially
> b. We are supposed to be watching for souls
> 2. "He that keepeth thy soul" — If He has saved us,
>   we ought to seek to win others

C. Thus God condemns our negligence
  1. We have not done what we should
  2. Our greatest failure lies in not possessing likeness
     to Christ
     a. We are to have it
     b. He was profoundly interested in winning the
        lost

IV. The Judgment of Negligence

A. This rendering to every man by works is conditioned
  1. It refers to the Christian
  2. It refers to rewards
B. Negligence has a bitter end
  1. Surely loss of reward (they shall suffer loss)
  2. Possibly something worse

Conclusion:

If you see someone going to death and do nothing, you are
responsible and judged before God. Will you seek to win someone for Christ?

Emotional Overdrive

PROVERBS 25:28

Introduction:

We live in a society without restraints. This is why we have to build even more in so many areas. One of the saddest and most common problems among God's people today is the problem of emotionally-driven folk.

I.   **The Meaning of the Passage**
   A. Identification of what is in view
      1. He is talking about the lack of self-control, of the ability to self-govern. Special focus is on those driven by feelings and emotions
      2. It is the other side of Proverbs 16:32
      3. Drawing a likeness — no self-control = city with walls broken down
         a. Dilapidated
         b. Defenseless
         c. Dispersed
   B. Illustrations of what it means
      1. Couple who want to walk with the Lord but always allow the old ways to draw them back
      2. Woman who wants to be what she should be but always allows moods to dominate
      3. Man who wants to serve the Lord but has no usefulness because of doubts based on feelings
      4. Young man doomed to a life of defeat and limitations because of inability to control temper (he is always ready prey, easily defeated, limited even when successful)
   C. The issue in view
      1. Emotions rule the intellect (feelings dominate the will)
      2. Because:
         a. It is the easiest way
         b. Patterns are all that way
         c. It feels good that way

3. The result: we do not know the meaning of victory; we suffer the loss of spiritual joy; we have broken relationships; we are a profound negative influence on the lives of others

II. The Message of the Passage
A. There are various solutions which can be proposed
   1. Take detailed steps
   2. Learn to channel anger, etc.
   3. Settle for less demanding Christianity
B. The KEY issue:
   1. A decision of the will is absolutely essential before relief can be found. There is no happy solution apart from a decision of the will
   2. You must determine what is going to run your life
   3. Once the decisions have been made, you can call upon the Lord for His help (which you must have before you can ever know victory)
C. The challenge: At what point will you stop waiting for magic to take over, and decide, with God's help, to turn things around in your life?

III. The Motivation of the Passage
A. It clearly calls for a decision on your part
   1. Nothing will happen until the decision has been made
   2. You must take the first step — then God will act to assist
B. It demands effort backed by the Spirit
   1. Cultivate self-control in matters of small moment in preparation for those greater
   2. Allow the facts of the Word to dominate your life
   3. Seek the Spirit's power to obey
C. Yield to Christ — some will not get saved because of feelings
   1. They are waiting for a special feeling
   2. They will not give up what feels good
   3. They feel they can not hold out. All you need do is what He has said to do

Conclusion:

You need not choose evil — just continue to yield to your feelings. To rule one's own spirit is to subdue an enemy that has vanquished conquerors. Who is in charge of your life?

A Dog By the Ears

PROVERBS 26:17

Introduction:
Virtually everyone knew about Lyndon B. Johnson (former President of the United States) and his hound dog. One article I saw on it quoted this passage, but the application was not right.

I.   **The Meaning**
      A. Translation:
         1. "Passeth by" belongs to dog rather than to "he that..."
         2. Should read: He that meddleth with strife that belongeth not to him is like one that taketh a passing dog by the ears
      B. It has a clear meaning
         1. Getting involved with strife that is none of your business is like grabbing a stray dog by the ears
         2. If you get involved in strife that isn't yours, it will be as big a problem as grabbing a stray dog (big problem may be how you are going to let it go)

II.   **The Manner:**
      A. Taking up another's offense
         1. Someone else has been offended or hurt, and you get involved in the situation
         2. This is very wrong
            a. You seldom know the whole story
            b. You take away the pressure on the person to do right
            c. You are not teaching the person how to handle offense situations
      B. Taking sides in a controversy between two people
         1. We are basically called upon to be peacemakers which is hard to do when you are positionalized
         2. This can only be done when we have fully heard both sides of the issue
         3. It is not enough to hear one person's version of the other person's side

C. Getting involved in a battle someone else should be fighting
   1. The issue that is involved in taking up another person's offense
   2. We should never do anything until the person involved has done what he or she should do about it
   3. We should not even listen to complaints about another person until that person has heard them
D. Getting involved with God's controversy with someone. This tends to take two forms
   1. Compromising with evil in an attempt to produce something right
      a. A wife's compromise with wrong will seldom result in her husband getting right
      b. A job given to reform someone will seldom work (although offering it may be good)
   2. Jumping into the fray when God is dealing with a situation
      a. Proverbs 24:17, 18
      b. Why should God take care of the matter if you are going to do so for Him?

III. The Message
Pointers to apply the message
A. There are situations that are indeed our responsibility
   1. We should only do so when we are sure
   2. We should do so prayerfully
B. There are many situations that simply are none of our business
   1. We should stay out of them
   2. We should stay *all* the way out of them
C. There are many who will try to involve us in situations we should not be in
   1. We must resist all their efforts
   2. We must try to get them to do what is right
D. We should never become involved in any strife until we are absolutely sure we know all the facts (Proverbs 25:8)
   1. We may make a bad situation far worse
   2. We may force someone to reveal facts that will hurt the person we are trying to help
   3. We may end up looking foolish in the whole thing

Conclusion:

God does want us to be involved in the lives of others. The Bible is full of instructions in that direction. It clearly spells out what and how. God does not want us to be involved in most strife and controversy unless we have specific reason to be so involved. Only get involved when you are backed by a specific Bible principle. Spend your time looking for things to stay out of rather than looking for things to get involved in.

Confess Your Sins

PROVERBS 28:13

Introduction:

It is an oversimplification to say that all the problems of life are the result of specific sin, but sin is a vital issue. This passage has some things to say to our problem.

I.   **The Folly of Concealing Sin — He That Covers It Shall Not Prosper**
     A. It results in living a lie much of the time
     B. It precludes forgiveness (1 John 1:9)
     C. It causes estrangement from God (Psalm 66:18)
     D. It produces inner problems
        1. An enormous weight of guilt
        2. Internal conflicts (Psalm 32:4, 5)
     E. It confirms sinful patterns
        1. Results in festering spread
        2. Produces repetition

II. **The Reasons for Concealing Sin**
     A. Ignorance — failure to realize nature of sin
        1. Insufficient knowledge of standard
        2. Failure to do what we know we should (James 4:17)
     B. No sense of need
        1. "I haven't done anything wrong"
        2. "Love covereth a multitude of sins"
     C. Too painful to face
     D. Too much pleasure involved to give up
     E. Too much pride to admit sin as sin

III. **The Answer to Concealment of Sin**
     A. Motivation
        1. The desire for forgiveness
        2. The weariness of suffering
        3. The desire for prosperity
     B. Steps
        1. Confession: agreeing with God that what we have done is sin (Psalm 51:4)

        a. This should be done in detail

        b. It should be done as soon as possible

    2. Forsaking

        a. It is absolutely essential

        b. It involves sorrow for sin

        c. It requires help from God

 C. Results

    1. The mercy of God is extended

    2. Peace of heart, mind and soul are made possible

    3. Prosperity is now potential (spiritual emphasis)

Conclusion:

We usually think of sin only in connection with the unsaved. It is important in that context, but it is also tremendously important for the Christian. It may be that unconfessed sin, unforsaken sin or a sloppy concept of confession are keeping you from spiritual prosperity.

No Vision

Introduction:
Sometimes the Scriptures are misused, especially by ignorance. Sometimes those who know the Bible well misuse it in certain places. Usually it is not serious, but rather a right truth from the wrong passage. This often makes us miss some good teaching. This verse is a case in point.

I.   **Corrected Interpretation**
    A. Common
        1. "No vision" — failure to see opportunity
        2. "People perish" — people are lost and go to hell
    B. Correction
        1. "Vision" — word which has reference to revelation (word refers to revelation of God's will through any agent)
        2. "Perish" — cast off restraint, become ungovernable
    C. Continuation
        1. The second part of verse 18 gives the clue to interpreting the first
        2. Meaning — "Where there is no proclamation of God's revelation, people cast off restraint and become ungovernable"

II.   **Challenging Implications**
    A. National sense
        1. This is probably the primary meaning of passage
        2. It is specially related to Israel, but generally true
        3. Illustrated
            a. Eli's time — no open vision (1 Samuel 3)
            b. Asa's days — Israel without a teaching priest (2 Chronicles 15:3)
    B. Personal sense
        1. Failure to hear and know God's Word leads to casting off restraint
        2. Failure to heed God's Word leads in same direction

C. Missionary sense
1. Comes back close to improper interpretation's meaning
2. Where the Word isn't proclaimed, things deteriorate
3. This lays responsibility on us

III. Corrective Indications
A. Contrast
1. The two phrases are designed to contrast with each other
2. The main premise
a. Where there is no proclaimed revelation, things are in a mess
b. Where God's Law is known and kept, there is happiness
B. Description
1. This really carries the whole matter one step further
2. Where revelation is known and obeyed, there is happiness
3. The nature of this happiness
a. Walking in path where the worst evils can not reach us
b. Living a life that will command respect and esteem
c. Abiding under the wing of the Father's favor
d. Expending our powers in happy service
e. Exercising benign influence in all circles
f. Traveling homeward
C. Implications
1. The law heard and heeded leads to salvation
2. The law heard and heeded leads to successful living
3. The law heard and heeded leads to true happiness

Conclusion:
"Where there is no proclamation of revelation, things deteriorate for individuals; but where the Word is heard and kept, there is happiness."

Two questions: Is it your fault that some people perish for lack of the Word? Could the state of your happiness reflect your relationship to the Word of God?

Things My Mother Taught Me

PROVERBS 31:26, 28

Introduction:

Mother was a great saint; a transparent Christian; a wise woman who attempted to build character. She was loaded with quaint old sayings. Some were funny: "Don't light three fires with one match;" "Woman taking last piece will be an old maid;" "Howling dog means someone will die;" "Black cat is bad luck." She had some of practical impact which were Bible-based or Bible-supported. We want to look at some today—

I. **Honesty Is the Best Policy (Ephesians 4:25, 28)**
   A. The Bible clearly teaches honesty
      1. Verbal honesty — it condemns lying
      2. Action honesty — it condemns stealing, cheating, etc.
   B. Society tends to wink at and expect dishonesty
      1. The criteria seems to be whether or not one is caught
      2. This carries over into Christianity
   C. The best policy
      1. For a nation — enormous cost of dishonesty
      2. For the individual
         a. It pleases God
         b. It frees from guilt
         c. It has its reward — whether or not it is tangible

II. **Two Wrongs Never Make a Right**
   A. The philosophy in view
      1. Being wronged by a person excuses a wrong in return
      2. It becomes a cover for a host of actions
   B. This is a common practice of society
      1. Our whole culture is pervaded by it
      2. Christians quickly pick it up
   C. The Bible's teaching is very contrary (Matthew 5:43-38; 7:12)
      1. Christians are always responsible to do right
      2. The conduct of another person never excuses me

III. **If It's Worth Doing At All, It's Worth Doing Well**
   A. This strikes at half-heartedness and shoddiness
   B. It is common in our society
      1. The desire to get by with the least possible effort
      2. An unwillingness to commit to anything
   C. The Bible strongly condemns it (Colossians 3:17, 23)
      1. The Christian ought to do everything well
      2. Things done for Lord especially ought to be well done

IV. **You Can Not Outgive God**
   A. A solidly-based Bible truth
      1. It is repeatedly seen in the Scriptures (Proverbs 3:9; 11:18, 24, 25; 19:17; 22:9)
      2. It is a specific promise of God
   B. It is often rejected
      1. Many withhold and know limited prosperity
      2. It takes faith to grasp!
   C. It is proven by experience. Everyone should try it out some time

V. **Strike While the Iron Is Hot**
   A. Symbolism involved
      1. From realm of the blacksmith
      2. Means to act when the situation is ripe
   B. It is a solidly-based biblical concept
      1. The Word calls us to act at once (2 Corinthians 6:2; Hebrews 3:7, 8, 15)
      2. The Word condemns failure to act — Israel at Kadesh-barnea; Agrippa (Acts 26:28)
   C. It has application in so many areas
      1. Some prompting to deed or act
      2. Some conviction of spiritual decision to be made!
      3. Salvation
   The longer any action is postponed, the more difficult it becomes to take it, and the more likely we are to lose!

VI. **Cheer Up: God Loves You**
   A. Real impact
      1. It has become trite
      2. It has great truth

B. Two applications
   1. To the child of God — rest assured that God cares
   2. To the unsaved — God loves you
C. Love demonstrated
   1. In sending Jesus so you could be offered salvation
   2. In sending the Spirit to move in your heart

Conclusion:

We live in a day of little character. Character involves likeness to Christ. God wants His people to show honesty, personal integrity (no matter what others do), whole-heartedness, generosity, prompt action. Most of all, God wants to save people. The most important decision you can ever make is that which concerns salvation.